ROSE O. SHARON

GOD
DELIVERS

A True Story

WESTBOW®
PRESS
A DIVISION OF THOMAS NELSON
& ZONDERVAN

Scriptures taken from the Holy Bible, New International Version®, NIV®.
Copyright © 1973, 1978, 1984, 2011 by Biblica, Inc.™ Used by permission of
Zondervan. All rights reserved worldwide. www.zondervan.com The "NIV"
and "New International Version" are trademarks registered in the United
States Patent and Trademark Office by Biblica, Inc.™ All rights reserved.

WestBow Press books may be ordered through booksellers or by contacting:

WestBow Press
A Division of Thomas Nelson & Zondervan
1663 Liberty Drive
Bloomington, IN 47403
www.westbowpress.com
1 (866) 928-1240

Because of the dynamic nature of the Internet, any web addresses or
links contained in this book may have changed since publication and
may no longer be valid. The views expressed in this work are solely those
of the author and do not necessarily reflect the views of the publisher,
and the publisher hereby disclaims any responsibility for them.

Any people depicted in stock imagery provided by Thinkstock are
models, and such images are being used for illustrative purposes only.
Certain stock imagery © Thinkstock.

ISBN: 978-1-4908-3843-4 (sc)
ISBN: 978-1-4908-3844-1 (hc)
ISBN: 978-1-4908-3842-7 (e)

Library of Congress Control Number: 2014909407

Printed in the United States of America.

WestBow Press rev. date: 5/29/2014

Contents

1. Voodoo..1

2. Childhood Abuse...7

3. Escaping Abuse... 13

4. Post-Traumatic Stress Disorder (PTSD)................... 21

5. God Pays Attention to Your Sorrows........................25

6. Why God Allows Trials................................ 31

7. Battles with Demonic Forces 37

8. My Conversion and Baptism.................... 45

9. God's Judgment..53

10. God Delivers I..59

11. God Delivers II..65

12. God's Amazing Miracles........................ 69

13. God's Immutable Love 75

14. Doubt is the Enemy of Faith................. 79

15. An Encounter with the Devil 85

16. My Bed of Affliction 91

17. God's Steadfast Promises........................97

CHAPTER 1

Voodoo

Do not tremble, do not be afraid. Did I not proclaim this and foretell it long ago? You are my witnesses. Is there any God besides me? No, there is no other Rock; I know not one. (Isa. 44:8 NIV)

Growing up as a child, I knew only the voodoo religion because everyone in my family practiced voodoo. At that time religion seemed useless. I hated the idea of serving the loas (voodoo spirit forces, similar to Catholic saints), and although I attended Catholic school, I also hated Catholics. In my village everyone worshipped the loas, yet every Sunday they were in the Catholic church. That was very confusing to me. I could not understand why people would do bad things all week and then go to church on Sunday. One thing I observed as a child was that many of the statues that devout Catholics paid homage to were also at the voodoo ceremonies but had different names.

As early as age eight, I refused to go to mass with my mom and siblings, and every Sunday I would get a spanking. I was different from my siblings. Unlike them, I could not tell a lie, not even to save my life. However, they seemed to find it very easy to tell a lie. I had seen how lies had destroyed other people's lives, so I took a stand to always tell the truth, no matter what.

Although I was never a participant in the voodoo ceremonies, my mother would often take me along with her. I watched the worshippers perform the various rituals, one of which was to feed the loas in exchange for special favors, which I felt demonstrated selfishness on the part of the deity. Many of the voodoo worshippers were very poor and could not feed themselves and their families, yet they had to provide the very best for the loas. The one thing I learned very early about the voodoo deity is that he was not merciful. He had zero tolerance for mistakes or disobedience. You had to do what he told you or else. Whenever he gave, he wanted something in return from you, sometimes a body part or a life. He was greatly feared by the worshippers.

There are many loas, as they are called, in the voodoo religion. In voodoo spirits are called loas, and each loa has its own personality, with likes and dislikes. At the rituals they were summoned by the priest or priestess and would take control of the person and speak and act through him or her. This possession is known as *mounting* or *riding a horse*, with the practitioner being the horse. Many of the worshipers lived in fear of the loas. There is also structure among the loas.

Back then I knew nothing about God, the true Creator, and how powerful and yet loving he is. In fact, when I discovered the true and powerful God, I was even more confused. You see, I could not understand how he could be so powerful yet permit evil to continue for such a long period. I could not see his love, and I had difficulty accepting him or believing he loved me. I often asked the question, "If this God is so powerful and loving, why doesn't he do something about all the suffering and pain that good people experience?"

I thought about my own life of suffering and pain. I was sexually, emotionally, and physically abused for fifteen years with no one to turn to for help. So where was this powerful and loving God Christians talked about? Why didn't he help me? Why did I have to suffer for so long? These are questions I have asked myself over and over again but with no answer. Since then I have found that there is only one God—who made heaven and earth and everything there is—and there is no other

God but him. I now know that God is merciful. Although my suffering and my pain were long and hard, I can truly say, "I am a survivor!" Yes, I am a survivor because God was with me in the midst of my suffering. My question now is, "How can a God so powerful also be so loving?"

In retrospect, I believe God was with me. In fact, I believe He was with me in the midst of my storms. My suffering was long and hard, but I endured, and in time God rescued me. I think of Job's experience and how Job asked for answers for his pain and suffering but instead received seventy-seven questions from God. Like Job, I am a survivor, and you can be a survivor too. Unlike Job, God has only one question for me and for you too: "Can you trust him one more time?"

Dear readers, remember that not all suffering is your fault. Yes, we do bring some suffering upon ourselves. Yet the innocent suffer too. Dreadful things happen—things we don't deserve, things that seem to be senseless. This is why God sides with the sufferer, and even when our minds tell us there is no hope, and our eyes are blind to hope, and our ears cannot hear hope—there is always hope. God experienced pain and suffering too on the cross, and every day he continues to experience pain when we reject him—the pain of a broken heart.

In his justice, God understands that this will seem unjust to you. He does not even try to give you answers because you could not understand. Instead, he visits you, as he visited Job. He is God—the great deliverer. He is the only possible answer. Though we find ourselves buried in a dark deeper than night, from the midst of the darkness, God speaks to us. The story of Job is not God's last word or last deed. Your situation, no matter how bleak it may seem, may be yet another deed for God. Another story to be written!

CHAPTER 2

Childhood Abuse

But by the grace of God I am what I am, and
his grace to me was not without effect. No, I
worked harder than all of them—yet not I, but
the grace of God that was with me. (1 Cor.
15:10 NIV)

It all started at a very young age: the sexual abuse, physical
abuse, and emotional abuse. At the age of ten, I was sexually
molested by my older brother. That night my life was turned
upside-down. It was a horrible nightmare. At the age of eleven,
I was again sexually molested by a neighbor. My mom had to

run an errand in the little town, so she left me with Ms. Adams. However, when Ms. Adams's husband came home from work, he molested me while his wife watched. He then threatened to kill my entire family if I told anyone. I lived with the guilt, shame, and fear every day. My life was without purpose. I became void of all emotions; I was numb inside. I was lost and discouraged, and life seemed daunting. I have often asked the question, "Why? Why me?" But I have never received an answer.

My mother became afraid for my life because she had gotten several complaints that I was always in the way of the loas. I did not like to go to church, and I was not respectful of the voodoo ceremonies. So when I was fourteen, my mother sent me to live with my father in the United States. When I heard I was coming to the United States, I was happy because I was to be given in marriage to a loa. Now please understand that this was not a marriage as we know it but rather a lifelong commitment of discipleship to the loa, just like Jesus and his disciples. The Devil has a counterfeit for everything God has instituted.

My dad took very good care of me when I was with my mom. I lived like a princess. People were paid to do everything for me, so I was very happy to come to America to be with him. Even though I did not really know my dad or have a relationship with him, I felt that since he took such good care of me when I was with my mom, things would be even better living with him. But I had a rude awakening when I arrived because there were no paid people to cook, wash, and clean for me. I had to do everything for myself.

My dad had a new wife and family, and things were not what I had expected. I had to quickly make adjustments to life's reality. Once I came to the United States, my father stopped sending support to my mom, so I started braiding hair to make a little bit of money to send home to my mom. My stepmom began to show resentment toward me, and she gave my dad an ultimatum to choose between her and his daughter, and he chose her. Finally I had to move out from dad's home and went to live with my paternal grandmother.

At my grandma's home, I was physically abused by my brother when I tried to intervene as he was beating his child with such brutal force. He then turned on me, and in the process my ear was damaged. Several weeks later I was in terrible pain because my ear became infected. I went to the hospital and was told I needed to have surgery. I was a minor so my dad needed to sign the consent form but he refused, and as a result I lost hearing in that ear.

While I was living with my grandmother, a man started visiting to teach us about the Bible. After my grandmother stopped taking Bible study, this man would still visit to give me Bible lessons. After a series of unfortunate circumstances, this man and I became sexually involved. He later became my husband and the father to my two children. When he first began to press me to be sexually intimate with him, I begged him to wait until I was at least eighteen so I could finish high school. But he refused. He told me that as long as we loved each other, in God's eyes we were already married, so there was no need to wait. I did not know where to go for help since my father had abandoned me, and after the incident with my brother, my grandmother also put me out. I had to fend for myself, so the saga of abuse continued.

But God had a plan for me because it was only by his grace that I have lived through and escaped from the abuse. Sometimes God will choose to deliver us through the storm or through the fire. Passing through the storm or the fire is painful, but God is always there with you. If you have survived a storm, please remember that you did not come through this because you are strong but only because God gave you the strength to endure. If you are in a storm or in the fire now, please know that you are not alone. Understand that you are being refined and that God has a purpose for your life. I am not saying that violence against women is acceptable; no, it is not. But God is able to take your bad situation and turn it into refined gold. Whatever your situation may be, you must believe there is hope.

Sure, it will appear that God is not there, and you may even doubt his existence and his power. But make no mistake—God does exist and he is powerful, but most of all he is a loving God. His ways I still do not understand, but God has said in his Word that his ways are not like our ways, and even his thoughts are not like ours. He is God. Who can understand him fully? We are not required to understand God 100 percent, but it is important to trust him 100 percent. Without faith it is impossible to please God!

CHAPTER 3

Escaping Abuse

No temptation has overtaken you except what is common to man. And God is faithful; he will not let you be tempted beyond what you can bear. But when you are tempted, he will also provide a way out so that you can endure it. (1 Cor. 10:13 NIV)

When I learned I was pregnant with my first child at the age of seventeen, I was scared. I thought to myself, *How am I going to give birth?* I had previously seen a documentary of a woman giving birth, and that image was stuck in my mind. Knowing that I would eventually have the same experience was more than my young mind could bear. When the child's father, Gary (not his real name), found out that I was pregnant, he gave me pills and teas in the hope that I would have a miscarriage. When none of his homemade apothecary worked, he took me to a clinic to have an abortion. But when I saw the baby's heartbeat for the first time during the sonogram, I could not go through with the abortion. When the father became aware of this, he very angry, and when we got home, the abuse began. He started beating me with the hope that I would have a miscarriage. But despite the physical and emotional abuse, I carried that baby to full term.

During my pregnancy Gary left for three weeks, and I didn't know where he was. Then he moved me to another state in an attempt to hide my pregnancy from his church to avoid being disciplined, and he would only come on weekends. Looking back I know God was with me because the only time I saw a doctor during my pregnancy was at the abortion clinic. I never receive prenatal care during my pregnancy because Gary would not take me to the doctor, and since he moved me to another state, I did not know my way around.

I remember when I started having labor pains, I did not know what it was, and Gary refused to take me to the hospital. He was afraid he would be arrested for statutory rape since I was underage. As the pain became unbearable, I began to cry, and he simply told me to shut up. But I was in so much pain I just continued to cry, and finally he took me to the hospital. But that hospital had no labor and delivery service, so I was taken to another hospital in an ambulance. But unfortunately for me the pains were not true labor; it was deemed a false alarm. Five days later, the same thing occurred. Again I was brought to the hospital, and three days later I had C-section. A beautiful baby boy was placed in my arms. My first thought was, *Wow! He is mine, and I get to keep him.* Those thoughts were short lived as Gary came in. He demanded that I tell the hospital that I did not want the baby and that he was not signing the birth certificate. In fact when the social worker asked if he was the baby's father, he quickly answered that he was my uncle. Gary wanted me to tell the hospital that I did not want the baby or my alternative would be to be homeless without him because he was not getting into trouble for me. I started to cry, and he told me to shut up because I could not cry at the hospital.

During my one-week stay at the hospital, I encountered some people from the Catholic church who gave me clothing, a baby bag, and other essentials that every new mother should have. When it came time to leave the hospital, Gary came and took me and the baby home. This was a great challenge for me. I was a young girl who had C-section with a newborn, and I had no one to help me with caring for the baby. I had to do everything for myself and my newborn. I cooked, cleaned, and did laundry. May I point out I had to hand wash the clothes, including Gary's, because we had no washing machine, and the Laundromat was not an option because it cost money.

I cried for many days because I had no food and no help. Sometimes I had to eat the baby's food so I could continue to breast-feed him. Gary did not want me to breast-feed my baby, so I would go in the bathroom and hide to just breast-feed my baby. It was a very difficult time in my young life. I felt that my life was over! I could not even see the tunnel, much less light in the tunnel. Those were long, dark days, and I often asked myself, *What did I do wrong? Where is that God that everyone talks about? Is he near or somewhere distant, only watching? If he is just and merciful, why is he not helping me?*

While I was in the hospital, after the birth of my son, I requested and was given the birth control shot (Depo-Provera). I chose the shot because Gary did not want me using birth control of any kind. To my dismay, two months later I found that I was pregnant again! I knew that if Gary was told, he would take me to the clinic again to have an abortion, and I knew that I could not and would not do this. So I waited until it was too late, and then told him that I had missed my period. Again he took me to the clinic to have an abortion. Nothing prepared me for what the sonogram revealed. The nurse told me that it was not a baby but babies! Yes, I was pregnant with twins. At that moment I became dead in spirit. I knew without a doubt that my life was over with three babies and an abusive man. There was no hope! Despite all of this, I still could not go through with the abortion, so when we got home, the saga of abuse continued. Gary grabbed my baby boy by his two legs, with his tender head hanging without any support. He threatened to kill us all.

After this tirade, he left for two months. I was pregnant with twins, with a newborn to care for, with no money, no food, no telephone, and the rent was not paid. I remembered when the landlord would come and knock on the door to collect his rent. I would stay very quiet and not answer the door and prayed that the baby would not start crying. Many a times I would leave him in his crib at nights so people wouldn't see me leaving without the baby and go outside and beg for money. I did not have a coat, so I was cold, hungry, and pregnant, and people were unwilling to give to a young pregnant girl. I felt that I was being judged by them, as no one stop to ask me why I was doing this. One day I went to the corner store, crying, and asked the cashier if could give me something to eat. May God bless him, because he responded by giving me bread, spaghetti, and a couple of other things. To this day, whenever I see someone begging on the streets, I cannot just go by and ignore them because I see myself in that person, and I remember where I came from. I will always stop and give what I can to help because I do not know what the person's story is.

One day I was able to use a pay phone to contact Gary's mother and found out that he was in jail. I was seven months pregnant then, and his sister took me to get Medicaid. I will always be grateful to her for doing this. When Gary got out of jail, his sister advised him to marry me now that I was of age so social services wouldn't ask too many question. After we got married, we lived with his mother. Now she began to verbally abuse me. She treated me and my son like we were thrash and underserving of her son. Many times she accused me of messing up her son's life. Gary continued to physically and verbally abuse me. Every week he would take his paycheck and gamble it all at Atlantic City.

I remember when my son was diagnosed with Type 1 diabetes, Gary, his mother, and his sister blamed me for this and called my son retarded. Gary told me that God was punishing me because I did not listen to him and have the abortion. At that point I thought, *Who is this God?* I felt that if he was not helping me then he might as well finish the job. What kind of God would punish someone for doing the right thing? I was hurting so much inside, and I had no one to turn to because I was cut off from my family and friends.

One day I asked Gary for money to buy milk for the babies, and he began to physically abuse me just for asking. His older brother, Allan, happened to stop by and saw my condition. When he found out what Gary had done, Allan proceeded to beat up Gary. After he left Gary took that rage out on me, and he physically abused me for three days straight. I was bruised all over, especially on my legs. His cousin came over, and when he saw my condition, he advised me to call the cops, which I did. The police then called Administration for Children Services (ACS). When they came and saw my condition, ACS immediately took me and the kids to a shelter. This was a shelter for women of domestic abuse, and it was the tunnel that I was looking for. All I needed now was to get to the end of this tunnel, and I hoped I would see the light there.

After two months in the shelter, I was given a two-bedroom apartment. The social worker gave me two cribs for the babies and told me about training to become a home health aide (HHA) and certified nurse assistant (CNA). However I wanted to become a medical assistant, and I was able to secure a partial school loan and financial aid in pursuit of this dream and career. This was the first ray of light I had seen in the dark tunnel of my life for a very long time. After I completed the medical assistant training, I was able to secure employment at a hospital, and I began to feel like there was hope after all for my kids and me.

It is at the darkest point in our lives that God breaks into the human scene and shines his light of hope. Second Corinthians

12:9 reminds us that God's power is perfected in our weakness. God's salvation is revealed to those who have no hope but God himself. If your days seem dark and hopeless, be encouraged that, "the Lord's hand is not so short that it cannot save; neither is His ear so dull that it cannot hear" (Isa. 59:1). If your situation seems hopeless and you are overwhelmed, cry out to God to save you. If you feel lost, in a tunnel of despair, then you are a candidate for his salvation.

CHAPTER 4

Post-Traumatic Stress Disorder (PTSD)

But the needy will not always be forgotten, nor the hope of the afflicted ever perish. (Ps. 9:18 NIV)

After I left the abusive man and his family, I was placed in a shelter for abused women. It was at this shelter that I began to experience flashbacks of the many traumatic events of my life. A flashback is the reality of reliving the pain of a trauma just as if it were happening in real time. After I experienced my first flashback, social services sent me to a psychiatrist for evaluation, and I was diagnosed with post-traumatic stress disorder (PTSD). PTSD is real for many victims of domestic violence. PTSD is an anxiety disorder triggered by exposure to a traumatic experience, such as physical or sexual assault.

During the period of abuse, my mind operated in survival mode, and sometimes it felt like I was not present. Now that I was no longer in the abusive situation, it seemed as if my mind was now processing the abuse and reacting to it. The flashbacks came involuntarily, and I had no control of them. This was very disheartening to me because when I was taken out of the abusive situation, I felt that finally it was over, only to find out it was not over. In fact I had a long road ahead of me—a road paved with weekly counseling and many strong medications. The medications I took seemed like a vicious cycle; for the basic functions of everyday living I needed some type of drug. I took medication for anxiety, which kept me awake, so I had to take one to sleep. The medication to make me sleep suppressed my appetite, so I had to take another one to eat. The medication lessened the occurrence of the flashbacks, and on stressful days I needed more medication. Life with those medications was very debilitating. It felt like my mind was never in the same place as my body as I was always so heavily medicated.

I stayed in counseling for two years without much progress as I still experienced the flashbacks and suffered with anxiety. Many times I just wanted to take my life to put an end to all the pain. But I thank God for my kids because they motivated me to stay alive. The thought of my kids suffering like I did was unbearable, and I felt that no one was able to take care of them like I did. I don't know how I did it, but I always had the energy to care for my children, but I could not take care of me. I took very good care of my children, but I gave them everything in abundance, which was my way of overcompensating for all the bad times. I felt I had to make up for all the times when my kids were abused by their father and I was not able to give them the basics of life, like food and clothes.

The Word of God tells us that the needy will not always be forgotten, nor will the hope of the afflicted ever perish. I was afflicted for fifteen years, but when I met my blessed Savior, what a difference it made! Many times I felt hopeless, that I would be better off dead, but Jesus gave me hope. Praise God my hope did not perish! After I accepted Christ as my Savior, I told God that I wanted to get off all medications, and in faith I stopped taking all of my medications. It has been one year now since I have been medication free. I must say that life on a daily basis is much better without medication. My body and mind are now cooperating with each other. The flashbacks and anxiety are gone! If you do not believe in miracles think again because God still performs miracles.

Friend, when you are broken, you cannot repair yourself. Let the divine surgeon of God, Jesus Christ, do the repairing.

Jesus identified with you and me so completely that he took the burden of our inward brokenness upon himself. He understands it all because he bore it all. By dying he took it to death, and by rising he opened a way through him to life. Despite the gloom in your life now, trust in God and his Son, Jesus, your price-payer, your sin-bearer, and through him give up your broken life and receive his own in its place. Can you trust him without reserve? Can you give up the ownership of yourself and transfer the title to God? If something in your heart is an obstacle—some fear, some pain, some pride—can you at least ask him to remove it? Our Father in heaven, please remove all obstacles in my heart now so I can trust you. In Jesus' name I pray. Amen!

CHAPTER 5

God Pays Attention to Your Sorrows

Record my misery; list my tears on your scroll—
are they not in your record? (Ps. 56:8 NIV)

Psalm 56 begins with David's cry for mercy because his enemies are attacking him. He implores the Lord to help him and to punish his opponents. Then, with striking imagery, David recognizes that God knows his suffering: "You keep track of all my sorrows. You have collected all my tears in your bottle. You have recorded each one in your book." David envisions

God writing down his sorrows so as to remember them. Do you know that God knows your sufferings, and he never forgets them? Yes, God knows how many times you have suffered. He keeps track of it.

Thus Psalm 56:8 not only reassures us that God knows our suffering but also reminds us of just how much we desire this very thing. When we are hurting, we want God to be aware of us. Of course we desire his help and healing. But almost more than this, we want to know that he is still there, that he knows and cares for us. The good news of Psalm 56:8 is that our God does indeed pay attention to our sorrows. Every cry, every tear, and every pain matters to God. Many people think that since God is so powerful, he cannot know suffering and sadness. While it is true that God is powerful, saying that he feels pain does not mean he is a weak God. Having feelings is not a weakness; it simply means he cares, and God takes advantage of the situation to make the best of it.

> But you have seen, for you observe trouble and
> grief, to repay it by your hand. The helpless
> commits himself to you; you are the helper of
> the fatherless. (Ps. 10:14 NKJV)

When sorrow has you, God knows what is going on. In fact he can even relate to it; if you are suffering over something you do not deserve, or if you grieve over a loss beyond your control, he is saying to you right now, "I understand your pain, my child, and I will give you my peace." Remember, God endures the loss of love all the time. Daily people are making the choice to follow him or to reject him. God leaves the choice up to the individual, and even though there is a promise of good things to come, some turn from his ways for sin. God loses these people, and it breaks his heart, for he loved them yet they rejected his love and his way. Try to hear his desire and his cry for Jerusalem in this passage of Scripture:

> Jerusalem, Jerusalem, you who kill the prophets and stone those sent to you, how often I have longed to gather your children together, as a hen gathers her chicks under her wings, and you were not willing. (Matt. 23:37 NIV)

Think about the love a mother hen has for her chicks. She keeps them warm under her wings, and as one family, they rest together. This is the kind of relationship Jesus says he wants with you. Not only does he want it now, but he says "Often I wanted ..." For a long time, he has desired this. "Yet the unwilling reject me." God knows pain and rejection. But he can take it, and he can deal with it. Yes, he can make it right and make the best of it. Be glad to be with him, for he knows your suffering, and he knows how to make it right.

Psalm 31 expresses beautifully God's compassion in relation to our suffering. Let us consider a few highlights from that passage:

> I will be glad and rejoice in your love, for you saw my affliction and knew the anguish of my soul … But I trust in you, LORD; I say, "You are my God." My times are in your hands; deliver me from the hands of my enemies, from those who pursue me … How abundant are the good things that you have stored up for those who fear you, that you bestow in the sight of all, on those who take refuge in you … Love the LORD, all his faithful people! The LORD preserves those who are true to him, but the proud he pays back in full. Be strong and take heart, all you who hope in the LORD. (Ps. 31:7, 14–15, 19, 23–24)

Even though you may see no escape from your suffering, God is saying to you, "I am here. I see and understand your affliction; you can talk to me about them, knowing I can relate. Come under my wing. Be strong, my child! Pray for wisdom, knowing I hear you and can answer. It is important to talk to me in the hard times, but most of all it is important to know I really do hear and can really relate. I love you with an everlasting love. I promise to never leave nor forsake you. We are in this together. Do not be discouraged. I am your Father, and I want what is best for you."

CHAPTER 6

Why God Allows Trials

Wait for the LORD; be strong and take heart
and wait for the LORD. (Ps. 27:14 NIV)

The question of why God allows trials is asked all the time.
Trials, although not pleasant, are necessary for many reasons.
Trials are necessary to every child of God because they act the
same way the refiner's fire purifies gold and silver. Yes, trials
remove impurities that sin has placed in our lives. Readers,
trials are not only like refiner's fire but also like DNA testing
to determine who our real father is. This is why trials are so
important in the life of every Christian; we need to know who

our real father is. Do you know who your father is? Sometimes God allows trials because the Devil incites/challenges him for our souls, just like in Job's case. There are times when it would seem like God has removed his hand of blessings from before us. In times like these we, like Job, must examine ourselves carefully. After this is done then we must be courageous and wait, yes, wait on the Lord.

The Word of God says in Romans 3:23 that we have all sinned, and the Devil uses this against the children of God. The Devil knows that "the wages of sin is death," but he forgets that "the gift of God is eternal life," so he does not care that God is merciful and forgiving. He accuses God of being unjust and knowingly protecting sinners so they can worship him. Therefore he challenges God to remove the hedge he places around his children and to remove his blessings so that our true nature/motives will be exposed.

The Devil cannot test or afflict you beyond what God has ordained for his perfect purpose and your benefit. When testing and trials come your way, you should receive them with joy because you know it is God who allowed them to strengthen your faith. When you are knocked about in the storms of life, like the tree that digs its roots deeper for a greater grip, you must dig your roots deeper into his Word so you can withstand whatever comes against you. Most comforting of all, always remember that God will never allow you to be tested beyond what you are able to handle and in all things will provide a way out of the test (1 Cor. 10:13). This does not mean he will remove the trial from you. Rather, the "way out" is the way through the trial, with God ever faithful by your side, until you come out on the other side of it by his grace and power, a stronger and more mature Christian.

Becoming a Christian will often require you to move out of your comfort zone and into areas you have never encountered before. You've heard the saying, "No pain, no gain" when exercising your physical bodies. The same applies to exercising your faith in God. This is why James wrote, "Consider it pure joy, my brothers, whenever you face trials of many kinds" (James 1:2 NIV). Testing your faith can be in small things like daily irritations; they may also be severe afflictions (Isa. 48:10). Whatever the source of the testing from God, it is to your benefit to undergo the trials. The account of Job is a perfect example of God allowing one of his saints to be tested by the Devil. Job bore all his trials patiently and "did not sin by charging God with wrongdoing" (Job 1:22). However, the account of Job's testing is proof that Satan's ability to tempt you is limited by God's sovereign control.

There are many examples that can be used to illustrate the positive results from you being tested. The Psalmist likens our testing to that of being refined like silver (Psalm 66:10). Elsewhere in Scripture you can read of your trials as that of gold being refined to remove all its impurities (1 Peter 1:7). By the testing of your faith, it cause you to grow and mature into strong disciples who truly live by faith and not by what you see (2 Cor. 5:7). When testing and trials come your way, you should receive them with joy because you know that it is God who allows them to strengthen your faith. When you are knocked about in the storms of life, take comfort in his Word so you can withstand whatever comes against you. Most comforting of all, you have the promise that he will never allow you to be tested beyond what you are able to handle and in all things will provide a way out of the test (1 Cor.10:13). This does not mean that God will remove the trial from you. Why would he when trials are for your benefit? Rather, the way out is the way through the trial, with him faithfully by your side, until you come out on the other side of it by his grace and power, a stronger and more mature Christian.

You may be facing a rough time right now—financially and emotionally—but if you trust God and keep on moving in faith he will make a way, even when you do not see a way. Trust him because he is able. Proverbs 4:18 says that the way of those who are righteous is like the early morning light. It shines brighter and brighter until the perfect day. Be patient; God knows what he is doing. He knows what is best for you. He can see the end result, but we cannot. All those problems, headaches, difficulties, and delays, everything that makes you ask, "Why?" will be clear one day—clear in the light of his love. Do you trust God? Readers, you can trust God, put him first in everything, and let him lead you "beside still waters." Remember that God will not give you more than you can bear and that he is always with you. He will give you the strength to persevere.

Sometimes things may seem so difficult. Just hold on to the calm assurance that God or our heavenly Father does deliver. Just like Daniel in the lions' den, he will rescue you. Trials will come and trials deeper yet, but God delivers. "Fear not when you pass through the water, I will be with you" (Is 43:2). The times you spend waiting in the darkness of your troubles will one day be rewarded by the Father of light. Sometimes God delivers us from our troubles, and sometimes he delivers us through our troubles.

Let all that we are wait quietly before God, for our hope is in him. He is our rock and our salvation. He is our defense. Be still before him, and wait patiently for him. God said blessed are those who mourn for they will be comforted. If you are waiting in the darkness of your troubles, be assured that God will deliver you. Be of good courage, and wait on the Lord! Yes, waiting is difficult sometimes, but what is the alternative to waiting for deliverance from a powerful God?

Friends, I had no reason to believe my situation would change, and even when God delivered me from the abuse, I still

Rose O. Sharon

faced the serious mental and emotional challenges that come with abuse. Many times I felt that I would not see another day, but God delivered me from those challenges also. God in his wisdom and power will make a way out for you. Never give up!

CHAPTER 7

Battles with Demonic Forces

I have given you authority to trample on snakes
and scorpions and to overcome all the power
of the enemy; nothing will harm you. (Luke
10:29 NIV)

Psalm 10:7 tells us that God is the strength of our salvation, and
in the day of battle, he will cover our heads. Yes, I can testify
that God has indeed covered my head in the day/night of battle.
My battle with demonic forces started when I decided to be
baptized and be a part of God's church. These forces of darkness
used my PTSD and my son's diabetes to control and scare me

into submission and to also reject God. But God supports the afflicted (Ps. 147:6).

Before I accepted Jesus as my Savior and was baptized, God placed five praying women in my life to help me fight in this battle. These women were prayer warriors and many times would spend all night tarrying in prayer. There were times when the demon would put me to sleep during prayer or I would have a near-death asthma attack. The demon would even challenge the women, but they resisted him through prayer, reading of the Word, and songs of praise.

One Saturday night one of the women received a text with instructions for me to get rid of a particular painting in my home. It was a painting of a man on a horse, which was given to me as a gift by my sister, but unknown to me, this man on the horse represented a loa. At first I was very reluctant to comply with the request, but my attention was removed from the picture to a loud thud coming from my son's bedroom. I quickly dropped the picture and ran to my son's room. I was shocked to see him lying on the floor unconscious. I started to cry as I related to the ladies on the prayer line what had happened. They told me this was a trick of the Devil to distract me from the task at hand. They assured me that as soon as that painting was out of my home that my son would be revive. There was no need for them to repeat that. I left my son on the floor and quickly ran toward the picture now lying on my living room floor; I was astonished to find a huge black spider on the painting. I grabbed a shoe and killed the spider, and immediately my apartment was plunged into darkness. All the lights went out, but as I looked out the window, I saw light in all of the surrounding apartments so I knew it was just my home.

At that moment my other phone rang, and it was my sister asking, "How dare you get rid of the picture I gave you?" How did she know what was taking place in my home? Now I became frantic. I wanted that painting out of my home. I went to the front door with the intention to take the painting to the incinerator, but as I looked through the keyhole of my door, I saw a strange man smoking a cigarette standing at my door. Please bear in mind that my son was still on the floor in an unconscious state, so I had to act quickly. But having to move in darkness was a great disadvantage. Nevertheless with God's help I was able to find a flashlight and a hammer, which I used to smash the painting into pieces, and then tossed it through a window. Once that was done, the lights came back in my apartment, and my son was also revived. I was so happy, the ladies were happy, and we were all giving God praise.

These godly women then advised me to go through my home and remove anything that was given to me or the children by my sister, and this I gladly did. The next day I saw a great improvement in my son's blood sugar, and from that day to now my son only takes two or three insulin shots a day instead of the fifteen shots. Hallelujah! God is indeed my strength, and he covers my head in the time of battle.

The Bible described the Devil as "like a roaring lion," but in reality he is not really a lion. Instead he roars like a lion with the sole purpose of intimidating his victims into fear. The Devil is a liar and a deceiver who uses deception as his weapon to gain advantage over those who are ignorant of the limitations of his power. The good news is that Satan has no rightful authority over believers! When Jesus gave his life on the cross as the sacrifice for the sins of the world, he also redeemed all of us from Satan's power. "For this purpose Jesus was manifested, that He might destroy the works of the devil" (1 John 3:8).

Satan is already a defeated enemy! His legal authority was neutralized by the finished work of Jesus on the cross. Every believer in Christ has authority over Satan. But the question is: if Satan is already defeated, why then is he still able to cause trouble? The answer is: because, although Jesus broke Satan's legal power, God has left it up to you and me to enforce the Devil's defeated condition. It's our responsibility to use the authority that Jesus has given us to put Satan in his place.

As believers we need not fear Satan but must exercise the authority God has given us over the Devil. Every person who is saved has been given authority over the power of the Devil. "I have given you authority to trample on snakes and scorpions and to overcome all the power of the enemy; nothing will harm you" (Luke 10:19 NIV). We have the right to use the authority of the name of Jesus to repel and drive Satan out of our territory and to break his grip over spiritual strongholds (2 Cor. 10:4). When we recognize Satan's activity and covert operations, we must take authority over him in the name of Jesus! Just as Jesus and the early apostles did, we must command Satan to leave (Mark 16:17). The Devil hates the name of Jesus and detests an atmosphere of praise and worship that exalts the name of Jesus. Jesus said, "For where two or three gather in my name, there am I with them" (Matt. 18:20 NIV). Be assured that the presence of Christ will expel the presence of Satan. Lifting up Jesus in praise will send the Devil running! Slam the door on the Devil!

However, it would be futile to order Satan's departure if we left the door wide open for him to flourish. The Bible warns not to "give place" for the Devil (Eph. 4:27). That is, provide no area of your life where Satan can be comfortable or establish strongholds. The Enemy can always be found working in those who entertain sin, disobedience, rebellion, or a self-willed nature. An unforgiving heart toward others is another area in which Satan flourishes (2 Cor. 2:11).

The Devil is watching you and me! When we fall into certain moods or we are overcome by various kinds of emotions, the Enemy steps in to defeat us—to lead us into sin. The wiles of the Devil include this cunning ability to find openings through our moods and emotions. Paul said, "Be angry, and do not sin: do not let the sun go down on your wrath, nor give place to the devil" (Eph. 4:26). When you are angry and take that anger with you into the next day and carry it along with you for weeks and months and years ... you might as well wear a bull's-eye. The Devil will find you and seek an entrance into your heart for his evil purpose you and to your downfall.

You must use the Word of God and prayer to take a careful inventory of your moods, your emotions, and the grudges we carry. Expel the hurt feelings you can't seem to turn loose of, the habitual, destructive thoughts you entertain. The Devil can use those things to slowly erode your character, to lead you into sin to gradually turn you away from God. Furthermore, any area of your life that is not submitted to God is considered open territory to the Devil, and he has the right to bring his expanding influence to those areas. This is why the Scripture says, "Submit to God. Resist the devil and he will flee from you" (James 4:7).

The only way to actually resist Satan is to submit yourself fully to God. This was what Jesus meant when he said, "The ruler of this world is coming, and he has nothing in Me" (John 14:30). Jesus had submitted himself to his Father, and although the Devil would try him, there was nothing for the Devil to use to gain an advantage. Rejoice! *You* have been given power over the Devil! By submitting to God and exercising your authority in the name of Jesus, you are more powerful than the Enemy. "He who is in you is greater than he who is in the world" (1 John 4:4).

Life will be difficult and challenging at times, and you may be so overwhelmed that you feel like you cannot continue on this journey of life. But don't give up! I have been there, and from my experience, there is always a way out. When you cannot find that way out, God in due course will bring that way out to you.

CHAPTER 8

My Conversion and Baptism

For it is by grace you have been saved, through
faith—and this is not from yourselves, it is the
gift of God— not by works, so that no one can
boast. (Ephesians 2:8–9 NIV).

My conversion and my baptism was an experience I will never
forget, for it was truly by the grace of God that I have been
delivered. Before I got baptized, as I have said before, I would
be on the prayer line with these women, and each time I was
attacked by the Devil, they would tell me to proclaim the name
of Jesus. But no matter how much I tried, that name would

never come from my lips. It was as if my jaws were locked down and my mouth was unable to open. The women told me if I proclaimed the name of Jesus, I would be released from the Evil One. I tried so hard to say the name of Jesus, but I could not say it. I even tried to write his name but to no avail. I am not quite sure what was really taking place and why I could not say the name of Jesus. I had no problem saying God's name; I just could not say *Jesus*. This went on for many weeks, night after night. I was being constantly tormented with flashbacks from my PSTD and with threats from my family members, who were all voodoo worshippers. Oh how I needed a break from all of this. I just wanted peace and a chance to be happy, but it seemed to elude me every time.

The women were faithful in prayer every night at 7:30 p.m., and I would join them. Then one Tuesday evening we started prayer at 7:30 p.m. as always, but that night I had flashbacks, and the women pleaded with me to proclaim the name of Jesus. It was very late, and we were all still on the prayer line, but this time the women seemed very determined not to get off the phone until I received deliverance. It was way past midnight, around 2:00 a.m., when they became tired, and as they had to work the next day, they decided to get off the phone. When the women got off the prayer line, I saw these two huge hands. I have never seen hands that big. It seemed as though the hands came through the walls, and they were placed on my head. The hands felt very warm but comfortable, and then I heard a voice telling me, "Say the powerful name of Jesus. Say the powerful name of Jesus." I did not have to be told a third time; I blurted out that name that I had been trying to proclaim for weeks. As I began to call out the name of Jesus, I felt the release, the deliverance, and the freedom that came. It was like a tremendous weight had been lifted. Hallelujah!

I sent the women a text message telling them that it was an SOS and I had to be baptized immediately. Needless to say we were back on the prayer line at 2:30 a.m. as I related to them what had taken place. Oh how they rejoiced. We stayed on the phone for the remainder of the morning. It was Wednesday, and I insisted that I had to get baptized that day. I was afraid that if I waited any longer, it would give the Devil an opportunity to try his tricks in order to stop my baptism.

At seven o'clock that Wednesday morning, my son started to bleed through his nose. The blood was just running. I did all I could to stop the bleeding, but it would not stop. I called Angela, one of the women from the prayer line and she called Carrie, and they both came on the phone and began to pray for my son. Just as my son's nosebleed began to subside, I began to bleed. I knew that this was not from my monthly cycle since I'd had my period the week before. The women asked me if I wanted to go to the hospital. I flatly refused because deep down I knew this was the trick of the Devil. So they continued to pray. Around ten o'clock Carrie received a text message that said that I was going to be okay and the bleeding would stop at eleven o'clock. I drew closer to the clock. My eyes were on the clock, and I refused to look away, fearing that I would not know when that crucial hour came. And sure enough at eleven o'clock the bleeding stopped. Praise God! I then took a shower and got dressed.

Meanwhile the ladies were able to contact the pastor, and he agreed to baptize me that day. I waited with bated breath as the clock ticked away the time. When I arrived at the church, there was a delay in getting the pool filled up, so the men began to use buckets to fill the pool. While waiting for the pool to be filled, I began to see things. Hideous demons were outside the church door that made me tremble. Nevertheless I was determined to be baptized.

The pastor stepped inside the pool, and then it was my turn and I hesitated. At that moment of hesitation, I began to fear that the water would be too cold, and many other thoughts came to my mind. Finally, after much encouragement, I stepped into the pool. The pastor prayed and then proceeded to immerse me in the water. While I was under the water, I felt like someone was choking me and I could not breathe. When the pastor brought me up from under the water, and as I stepped out of the water, I passed out because I could not breathe.

As I lay on the floor of the church, the same huge hands and the same voice I saw and heard the night before appeared, and this time the voice said, "Enough." The big hands took both of my hands and put them together in a prayer formation, and at that moment, I opened my eyes. What I saw was amazing; the entire church was filled with a bright light. The light was so bright that I could see nothing else but light from the ceiling to the floor and from wall to wall. When I came to myself, I had terrible pains on both sides of my neck, and I knew an attempt was made on my life by the Devil, but for the mercy and grace of a loving God, he did not succeed.

My journey after my baptism was extraordinary. There were many struggles and battles with evil forces, but my faith remained steadfast. The day after my baptism, I began to hear a voice repeating passages of Scripture, telling me Bible stories. This was strange because I did not know whose voice this was. It was the most beautiful voice I have ever heard. The voice seemed to go with me everywhere. I feared I was losing my mind. One day I sat in a park for four hours, and for the entire period of time, I heard the voice. I began to text what I heard to Angela, one of the praying women, and each time I would asked her if these things were true and in the Bible. Her answer was always the same; yes, these things are true and are in the Bible. I asked her whose voice it was and what these things meant. They all agreed that this could only be the voice of God speaking to me.

One morning a very bright light came into my room, and it filled the entire room. This light was warm and comfortable, and a voice from the light said, "Fear not. I am that I am." I then asked, "Who is I am that I am?" The voice replied, "You will learn soon." Since then I have learned that God is I am that I am. Much happened after my baptism, and there were many changes, but the one thing that remained constant was that at six every morning this light comes into my room, calls me by name, and then proceeds to read from the Bible and often times teaches me songs. This is also repeated at night when I am ready to go to bed. The voice would read to me and then say, "Rest, my child," and I would immediately fall asleep and always wake up refreshed the next day.

I often wondered why so many people did not want God in their lives. If they would just give God a chance, they would realize how loving God is. God is like a giant onion with many layers, and each layer represents a trait in his character. God is very respectful of our decision; if we do not want him in our homes and our lives, he will leave. That is why the Bible says he "stands at the door and knock" (Revelation 3:20). He will not stay where he is not welcomed.

When we reject God in our lives, it breaks his heart the same way we are broken when we are faced with rejection.

Remember that we are made in God's image. Therefore we should expect to see similarities in the characteristics of God and man. Many see God as an exacting judge looking over our shoulders to punish us when we do wrong, but this is far from the truth. God is merciful and compassionate, and believe it or not, he does have a sense of humor. More than anything else, God wants our companionship. He wants to talk to us like good friends do; he wants us to talk to him about our joys, our sorrows, and our plans. But so many times we have failed to trust him and we have "leaned on our own understanding," only to find ourselves hitting rock bottom and looking up into his face.

I have only been walking with God for a short period of time, but I love him. I have no doubt in my mind that he loves me, and I know he loves you too. Yes, you may have been abused and abandoned by those who were supposed to love and protect you, and it may even seem like God is looking the other way. But he is not. You are his child, and he has promised never to leave nor forsake you. Why not talk to him right now and feel the change? Don't wait until you are more presentable to come to him; go to your Father now. Tell God what is in your heart, and remember it does not matter where you have been or what your have done or even what you have had to endure. God loves you and will always forgive you. Don't wait!

CHAPTER 9

God's Judgment

You have exalted my horn like that of a wild ox; fine oils have been poured on me. My eyes have seen the defeat of my adversaries; my ears have heard the rout of my wicked foes. (Psalm 92:10–11 NIV).

When I look back on my life, this passage of Scripture takes on new meaning because I have seen the defeat of my adversaries, and I have had fine oils poured on me. I have seen those who were against me or mistreated me defeated by God. I have also experienced God's grace in my life, and it is indeed like fine oils being poured on me. One thing we should always remember is that vengeance is not ours to repay, but it is God's. He is in control of our situation, and he will work it out according to his will.

When I told my family I was going to get baptized, they were livid and tried everything, including force, to prevent me from being baptized. But I was determined to go through with the baptism. My dad and siblings were very mean to me, and they harassed me every chance they got. They just could not understand why I would choose to be a Christian. They went to great lengths to stop me from going to church. My dad threatened me that if I continue to attend church, he would disown me as his daughter.

One day my sister came to my home and saw a Bible and a set of Bible studies; she went bananas and proceeded to rip apart both the Bible and the lessons. It was very upsetting to me to watch her treat the Word of God with such disdain. At that point I could not control my emotions, and I punched her. That day my sister and I fought. The disturbance alerted one of my neighbors, and the police were called. When the police officers arrived, they arrested my sister, and she was charged with damaging private property and endangering the welfare of minors. In court my sister was fined a small amount by the judge for damaging the Bible. As of the writing of this book, my sister still has a case pending in the court for endangering the welfare of minors. My older sister was admitted to a mental hospital after she attempted suicide. This situation brought the wrath of my entire family on me. One evening after I picked up my kids from school I was astonished to find the entire gang in front of my door. They would not allow me and my children to enter my own home. They blocked the door and insisted that I go with them to the mental hospital to take the place of my sister. They told me she should not be there and that I was the one who should be in the mental hospital. I had to get away from them because I did not want to subject my kids to that kind of behavior. I took my kids by the hand, and I started walking away from my family members. As I was walking, I called my friends Rachel, Carrie, and Angela to let them know what was taking place and to solicit their prayers for the situation.

It was a very cold evening, so I decided to take shelter from the cold at a nearby hospital. It was there that I received a call from Rachel telling me that she got a text from God with instructions for me to go home. I wasted no time in heading back home. As I got closer to my apartment, I saw a police squad car parked in front of the building. My heart was racing, and I began to shake as I saw two officers handcuff my dad and put him into the car. To this day I do not know who called the police. My brother was holding the lobby door wide open and there was no one else in the lobby, yet my kids and I went through those doors without my brother or the other family members seeing us. The elevator door opened immediately, and we were able to get home safely.

On another occasion my friend Angela took the day off to fast and pray for me because I was having such a hard time coping with the constant harassment from family members. I had had enough and I just wanted peace, but peace seemed to be elusive. However that day she called me in the afternoon. At first I ignored her call, but she would not give up, so I took her call. She told me she had gotten a text instructing her to call me with her Bible in hand. That afternoon I was given a Bible study by the voice from the light.

We were just about finished with the Bible study when I received a phone call from my mother. The information she related to me was horrific. She told me that our neighbor was burned to death in his own home. This was the same neighbor who had molested me when I was ten years old. While I was recovering from that news, I received another call, this time from my sister. Again it was horrific in nature. My brother—who also molested me—was shot in his private parts by an enraged father who caught him in the act with his ten-year-old daughter. After that second call, I became concerned for the life of my father. I asked my friend Angela to pray and asked God to stop his judgment. I was very angry with all of the people who hurt me, but I did not want them dead.

Angela was in shock. Things were happening quickly, and this was all news to her. While I was begging her to ask God to stop, I got yet another phone call. This time it was about my Grandma; she had a stroke and was in the hospital. I was now frantic and broke down in tears as I received yet another phone call telling me that my dad and my stepmom were both in jail and my brother was in the hospital with stab wounds. At this point I cried out from the depths of my

heart, "God, please stop! I forgive them all." God's outstretched hand was drawn back, and I felt like the *Titanic* was lifted from over me. I felt only peace—God's peace! My eyes had seen the defeat of my adversaries; my ears had heard the rout of my wicked foes.

This experience taught me that the battle is truly the Lord's, and he will fight the battles for his children. Sometimes we allow pride to get in the way, and we want to take matters into our hands. I have been there, and honestly God's way is always the best way. We may not always understand his ways, but his thoughts are not like ours neither are his ways like our ways (Isaiah 55:8). It is important to trust God and allow him to work things out according to his will and for his purpose. Yes, sometimes it may seem like God is taking a long time to come to your aid, but I have learned wait on him. It is important to have a relationship with God; only when we have a relationship with God are we able to trust him. It is when we trust God that we are able to let go of the controls and turn it over to God.

Fear not; God will be with you in the fire of your circumstances, and he is able to deliver you. Be patient. Your deliverance will come!

CHAPTER 10

God Delivers I

Though you have made me see troubles, many and bitter, you will restore my life again; from the depths of the earth you will again bring me up. (Psalm 71:20 NIV)

When God delivers, you will know without a doubt that it is indeed the God of heaven. I have experienced God's deliverance several times. The first time was when I accepted his Son as my personal Savior. Before my conversion, I was involved with a group of praying women—Carrie, Rachel, and Angela—who were not afraid to tarry in prayer, sometimes for a whole night.

They were praying for me and with me, but the accuser of the brethren, the Devil, would battle ferociously with us. They refused to let him have me.

These ladies believed in the true and living God, and they also believed he would deliver me just like he did Daniel in the lion's den. They felt my pain, my despair; when I cried, they cried with me. But they would not give up. They told me to rebuke the Devil and claim deliverance in the name of Jesus, but there was something about that name that I could neither speak it nor write it. Until one night after praying with the women until two o'clock in the morning, God himself paid me a visit when he touched me with his mighty hands.

Yes, God himself, touched me on my head and asked me to say the powerful name of his Son, Jesus. Oh, I am so glad he did! Now Jesus is the sweetest name that I know. After that night I knew that I could never turn back, but there was so much more that I needed to know about God and his Son. As mentioned before, I was confused about the ways of God. I did not understand why God seemed to take so long to execute his judgment over evil. But now I know that it is because he is merciful. I also know that he will protect his people, as I have experienced his protection on many occasions.

One early morning I got a phone call from one of my dear sisters in Christ. It was 5:30 a.m., and I was not happy to be awoken by the caller, so I hung up on her, but she persistently called again, saying she had a very important message for me. What she told me sent shock waves through my entire body. My sister told me that she received a text from God to warn me, "Whatever you do today, do not go to your friend Jasmine's house because her boyfriend is going to drug your coffee and then rape you." I was appalled by that message and also astonished because my caller did not know I had plans to go to Jasmine's home that morning. But Jasmine was a very good friend, so how could that be? Was she aware of this?

While I mused about this situation and what I should do, I got a call from Jasmine telling me that she and her boyfriend were on their way and she was bringing me my favorite drink: coffee. Why were they coming? The plan was that I would go to her house on my way to work. I took my child to school, and as I got to the train station, I saw them, but they did not see me. I jumped on the first train that came, but this train was going in the opposite direction of my job. When I finally got off the train, I simply walked around for hours in the cold, as this was November, before getting on another train heading home. By then I was very upset because I had to call out from work, and I was running around like a fugitive in the cold. With much ostentation and determination, I decided to go home and deal with the situation. As I was walking toward my apartment building, I saw Jasmine, with the cup coffee still in her hand, and her boyfriend in front of my building waiting for me. I was shaken by this because this drama started to unfold at around 7:30 a.m., and it was now 2:30 p.m. I was cold, tired, and furious, so I went to the nearby park to sit down as I contemplated what to do.

What happened next was like something out of a movie. I saw a police car driving down my block, and it stopped in front of my building. The police officers got out and handcuffed both Jasmine and her boyfriend and drove off with them. My mind was racing, and my body was shaking! Who called the cops? Why were they arrested? Later on I received a called from Jasmine's mother informing me that her daughter and her boyfriend were in jail. Cocaine was found in the boyfriend's possession. The case went to trial, and Jasmine was sentenced to six months and the boyfriend one year in prison.

This incident taught me the power of divine intervention and the love God had for me. You see, dear readers, if this evil plan was allowed to take place, it would have been a terrible setback for me. As a victim of sexual abuse so many times in the past, I had reached a critical point in my life. But today I give much praise and thanks to the God who delivers because I am no longer a victim but a survivor.

Never forget that through all our supplications and prayers, our heavenly Father surely hears. He knows, and he answers. When it seems that you cannot stand and no hope is shown, do not doubt because he would not put more on you than you can bear. He will give you the strength to persevere. Sometimes things may seem so difficult. Just hold on to the calm assurance that our Father does deliver. Just like the three Hebrew boys in the fiery furnace, he will rescue you. Trials will come and trials deeper yet, but God delivers. "Fear not when you pass through the water, I will be with you" (Isaiah 43:2). The times you spend waiting in the darkness of your troubles will one day be rewarded by the Father of light. Sometimes God delivers us from our troubles, and sometimes he delivers us through our troubles.

CHAPTER 11

God Delivers II

Before they call I will answer; while they are
still speaking I will hear. (Isaiah 65:24 NIV)

God is no respecter of persons, and he loves all of his children.
The following two testimonies tell of God's love and mercies
toward us. It was back in April that God came to me and said
he had a special appointment for me in two weeks. I wondered
what it was. Two weeks later, God came on a very brisk spring
morning. It was a Sabbath day. After my baptism God visited me
as a bright light that filled my entire room. On this particular
morning, he asked me to get dressed and follow him. So I did!

I followed the light to the elevator and then through the lobby of my building to the outside, where a yellow cab was waiting. The light got into the cab, and I followed. I gently closed the door as the cab driver drove off.

After driving for a while, the car finally stopped in front of a house. The light got out, and I did the same. Soon we were at the front door and I was told to knock on the door, but there was no response to my initial knock. He said it again, so I knocked again. This time the door swung open, and a very young mother stood at the door.

"Can I help you?" she asked.

"No, but I came to help you," I responded.

At this point she invited me in. To say the least, she was astonished because she did not know me. I introduced myself to her and told her that God sent me there to help her. She shared her story with me.

Alice was a young mother with a three-month-old baby. The man who fathered her child had walked out on her and the baby that Friday, leaving her with no money for rent, food, or diapers. She became very despondent, and when I knocked the first time, she was about to suffocate the baby and then take her own life. It was at that very moment that God told me that there was four thousand dollars in my pocket and to give it to Alice. She could not believe it! We went food shopping and also bought what the baby needed. When we came back, I cleaned the apartment and cooked for her. I also shared my story of having to fend for myself and my children when I escaped from their abusive father. The two of us bonded, and to this day we are still in touch.

Today Alice has accepted Jesus as her personal Savior and relocated to another state to live with relatives. She has witnessed to that family, and they have also accepted Jesus into their lives. Alice is now currently employed, and as of the writing of this book, she is in school studying to be a nurse. Alice did not believe that there was a God, let alone one that loved her. What a wonderful and powerful testimony of God's love and deliverance.

This next story is one that demonstrates God's tender mercies and the power of faith. One morning as I was leaving for work, God showed up and asked me to follow him. As always I asked no questions; I just followed the light. Why? Because I have faith in a living, powerful, loving, and personal God. So I followed the light to the train station and onto a train going uptown. Yes, God rides the city subway! We were on the train for about thirty minutes before we got out at the designated stop.

The light walked to the front door of a home, and I followed. I was about to ring the doorbell, but the voice said, "The door is open." I slowly opened the door and stepped inside and immediately heard groans. I quickly headed to the area where the groans were coming from, and there on the bathroom floor was an elderly woman. My heart ached for her. My thoughts and emotions were interrupted when I heard her ask me if I was her angel sent from God to help her. She told me that she prayed all night for God to send an angel to help her. Joanne had so much faith. She did not give up; she was in pain and spent the entire night lying on a cold floor with very little to cover her body. I attended to Joanne, checked her blood sugar, called 911, and made sure she was dressed. As we waited for the medics to arrive, she explained to me that as she was coming out of the bathroom after taking her evening shower, she fell and was not able to get up.

When the ambulance arrived, Joanne was taken to a nearby hospital, where she was hospitalized for several weeks. After her recovery, Joanne's daughter took her to live with her. I admire her faith in God, for there was no doubt in her mind that God would deliver her, and he did. What an awesome God! When life is difficult, remember that God is just a prayer away. Nothing that happens to his children takes him by surprise, and he is never shocked by our situation. But we must have faith in God!

CHAPTER 12

God's Amazing Miracles

So he cried out to the Lord, and the Lord
showed him a tree. When he cast it into the
waters, the waters were made sweet. There He
made a statute and an ordinance for them, and
there He tested them. (Exodus 25:16–17)

As I said before, my first miracle from God was my deliverance
and transformation. But he still continues to perform miracles
every day of my life. Another one of his miracles that I have
experienced happened at a bus stop. I heard him clearly say to
me, "Go to that garbage bin and you will find a bag inside.

You are to open the bag." I obeyed, and there was a one hundred–dollar bill inside. I remembered how excited I was, but as I turned around to leave, I saw an old woman who told me that she was hungry. I took her to a nearby restaurant and bought her something to eat and then gave her twenty dollars. Altogether I had dispensed of thirty dollars and had seventy dollars left. However, when I got home I was told that because I was kind to the old woman, there was now two hundred dollars in my pocketbook. Well I checked my pocketbook, and to my great surprise, there was indeed two hundred dollars there. I was shaking, not from fear but from an overwhelming joy that this powerful God would even consider me to experience this amazing miracle.

Let me share another miracle that God performed, one of which if he had not done at that time would have destroyed my faith in him. As was my custom, I would give literature to pedestrians as they passed by, so this day in question was no different—that is until I got home and realized I had left my pocketbook on the train with a sizable amount of money in it and all my credit cards and my debit card. Oh, I was so angry with God; I felt that after doing his work the least he could have done was remind me to take my pocketbook as I was getting off the train. I cried myself to sleep that night.

But you see God had other plans for me, like he said in Jeremiah 29:11, "For I know the thoughts that I think toward you, says the Lord, thoughts of peace and not of evil, to give you a future and a hope." When I arrived to work the next day, one of my sisters in Christ called me. What she said had a profound effect upon me. She told me that I would find my pocketbook where I left it. You see, I did not tell this dear sister what had transpired the day before, so I was shocked that she knew. She also told me that I would find the bag on my way home from picking my kid up from school, with everything intact. She said God needed me to believe and so I believed. Remember, this was public transportation and twenty-fours later.

That evening, after picking my child up from school, I went to the train station to wait for the train to go home. When the train arrived and the doors were opened, to my dismay, it was packed. I thought to myself, *God is it possible for a train packed with the rush-hour crowd that no one saw that bag?* As I stepped into the train, I noticed a pregnant woman standing in front of the empty seat I had occupied the previous day. Readers, God is good all the time because there was my bag on the empty seat. I slipped right in and sat down while discretely taking what was mine. I searched the bag for fear my valuables were gone. But to my astonishment everything was intact, even the money. Trust in the Lord always!

On another occasion, while I was in a grocery store, I observed a woman with a toddler in a stroller. She was just walking up and down the aisle of the grocery store, looking very distraught. I wondered what was wrong. Then I heard God say to me, "Go to the freezer section and open the door." As always I obeyed. Nothing prepared me for what I saw when I opened the freezer door. God said, "Take the money and give it to the woman with the baby in the stroller." It was $250! I approached the woman and asked, "Can I help you?" She said to me that she only had ten dollars and she and the baby were in need of so much and everything was so expensive that she could not decide what to purchase. I told her to go ahead and get all she needed. She got a shopping cart and filled it with food items and diapers for the baby. We proceeded to the cashier, and after every item in her shopping cart was scanned, the total was $250. I gave her the money to pay for her groceries. She could not believe that a perfect stranger would offer to help her. I told her that it was God's way of showing that he loved her. She wanted to know if I was an angel.

Another time I was at Western Union to pay a bill when I noticed there was a woman standing in a corner crying uncontrollably. I approached her and asked if I could help her. She then explained to me that she owed six months' rent, and a friend had promised to meet her there to give her a loan to pay the rent. But when the friend did not show up, she called her, and that was when she learned her friend was not coming and had changed her mind about the loan. Immediately God said to me, "Tell her to follow you," so I did. God led me to the ATM of my bank and then told me to withdraw the amount for the rent owed, so I did. I gave the woman the money to pay her back rent. She was shocked. She asked me about repaying the money, and I told her, "Don't worry about it." I waited one week and then checked my account. Believe it or not ... my account never showed that money was withdrawn. Yes! There was no record of any withdrawal of the amount I gave the woman to pay her back rent. All I can say is God is good!

The next miracle I would like to share with you is the night my son died. My seven-year-old son has Type 1 diabetes and has had it since he was a toddler. On this night in question, I fed him and checked his blood sugar, which was 184, and put him to bed. I was just about to pray when I heard my son scream. I rushed to his room, and he was shaking like he was about to have a seizure. I checked his blood sugar, and it was at 42. I could hear the ladies on the prayer line praying, but instead of his blood sugar going up, it began to drop rapidly. His blood sugar went from 42 to 15 and then 14. At this point my son had stopped breathing and turned blue. I knew he was dead; he was dead for seven minutes. I then prayed a prayer of faith.

You see, past experiences taught me that this was the trick of the Devil. He was using my son again to break my relationship with God. But it was at that moment that I made my determination that this harassment from the Enemy had to stop. I told God that I was sick and tired of fighting with the Enemy, that I would not call 911, even it meant spending the rest of my life in jail. I would still praise him and tell others of his wondrous love. That night I decided to wait on God's will, whatever it was. Yes, I know that sounds foolish for a mother, but I know my heavenly Father. After waiting what was the longest seven minutes ever, my son started to cry just like a newborn does. I again checked his blood sugar, which now read a perfect 120.

As I held my son in my arms and comforted him, I knew the life giver was in the room, and he had raised him up. Readers, all things are possible with God. Don't give up; he has promised to be with you in the fire. He is able to turn your bitter trials into sweet testimonies and your mourning into joy. He still continues to this day to perform his amazing miracles in my life. Life with the true Creator God is truly exciting. There is never a dull moment. Yes he loves me, and he loves you too!

CHAPTER 13

God's Immutable Love

For God so loved the world that he gave his one
and only Son, that whoever believes in him shall
not perish but have eternal life. (John 3:16 NIV)

Do you think God is far away and only concerned with your
good deeds? Do you think he loves people who grew up in a
Christian home more than people who didn't? Do you think
you have done things *so* bad that he can't possibly truly forgive
you? Then you are the person God wants to speak to. He
wants you to know who he really is so that you will trust him
and experience eternal life—both now and forever! Jesus said,

"Now this is eternal life: that they may know you, the only true God, and Jesus Christ, whom you have sent" (John 17:3 NIV). Our heavenly Father cares very deeply about each of his children. The desire of his heart has always been to be in communication with us, but sin got in the way and has been like a veil between God and us. To communicate with us, that veil must be torn, and that is what Jesus, his Son, did on the cross. Jesus removed the veil so we can communicate to a loving Father through Jesus. "No one comes to the Father except through me" (John 14:6 NIV).

Throughout God's Word, God is depicted as a God who wants a relationship with his people. He is the one pursuing that relationship. Just like a young man desperately in love with the girl of his dreams will do anything he can to spend time with that lovely girl, God pursues you, hoping he can spend time with you. God, our Creator and Father, is a God of love and demonstrates that love to his children in many ways. Sending his Son to Calvary to take the place of sinners was the ultimate sacrifice of his immutable love toward us. We have a choice to make; we can accept God's invitation to have a close relationship with him and enjoy that relationship beyond the world's imagination, or we can just continue to wander about and stay the way we are, in a lukewarm, comfortable environment, and just proclaim we know God exists. But knowledge will not set you free!

When we experience pain and sorrows in our lives it does not mean God has forsaken us or no longer loves us. On the contrary, he is in the midst of our pain and suffering, and his love is shown through those difficult times in our lives. He said that he disciplines those whom he loves. John 3:16 says God so loved that he gave. You see, God demonstrates his love by giving, and his love does not change. The principle of love is to sacrifice self for others. Yes, God wants to save all of his children so he gave his only Son, Jesus, on Calvary. But you may ask, why the sacrifice? Jesus showed the Father that he loved him perfectly when he submitted his will to the will of the Father. It is easy to say, "I love you," But it is through sacrifice that love is actually lived and shown, just like Abraham did on Mount Moriah when God commanded him to offer up his only son, Isaac, as a sacrifice.

Our perception of God is flawed, and our understanding of him is too narrow. We limit God when we think of him in the human realm. He is not like man, but man must be like him. God is not like man because he has no limit. He cannot be put in a box or a closet. He cannot be confined to any one deed or even thought. He works best when he is not restrained by man. His love is best understood when we trust and obey him. Jesus came so we can experience the fullness of God's love. Yes, God is not like man, but man must be like him. Jesus, our example, came to show us how to be godly in our thoughts, words, and actions. We must be like Jesus all day long, in our homes, on our jobs, and in our communities. Jesus prayed in John 17:11 that we will be one with him, even "as he and the Father are one."

The immutable love of God knows no prejudice and it is like the ocean; the more he gives, the more there is. He comes seeking for us when we are lost, and when sin bears us naked, he covers us with his grace. When guilt and shame condemn us, he grants us mercy. Although we deserve nothing from him yet his immutable love offers us everything. God is an awesome God!

Sometimes I do not understand why God's heart yearns for us—why he would send his only Son to come to this sinful world to die such a horrible death for you and me. John 3:16 tells us that God gave because he loved. The truth is, God has done all he can possibly do to demonstrate his love for a wayward people; we must now do our part and respond to the love of God. He has promised us eternal life if we believe. How will you respond to the love of an awesome God and father?

CHAPTER 14

Doubt is the Enemy of Faith

By faith the walls of Jericho fell, after the army
had marched around them for seven days.
(Hebrews 11:30 NIV)

I have learned that doubt is the enemy of faith and trust. It is a
spiritually destructive force that tears us away from God. God
wants to lead us on a journey, but he must have full control of
our lives. Remember, God is for us, not against us. Sometimes
God has to put us out of our control so we can learn to trust
him. He wants us to have something deeper and harder than
belief or faith: trust. We can only trust when we have let go

completely and let God be in control. When we learn to trust God out of our emptiness, when we let God in more deeply, when we surrender all and trust, we become liberated from our doubt, wondering, and fears, and we learn to live with freedom and joy; when we learn that all things are possible with him, when we let all our thoughts be captive to him and that he is shaping everything together for our good; when we believe that he will see us through any adversity so that we will not just make it through but we will overcome it—then and only then have we learnt to trust! Don't let circumstances ruin your trust.

There were many times when I had to exercise trust in God. One Sunday morning he came into my room and asked me to follow him, but following God was not the issue that morning. The issue was until then was that I always took my children with me to do his task—literature distribution. But on this Sunday morning he told me to leave the kids home and he would take care of them. I asked him if he would send one of his angels to be with them. He said no, he would be there with them. I am a single mom and I never leave my children at home; they go everywhere I go. I had to make a difficult decision to trust and obey God or decline. But how could I say no to God? I called Carrie and Angela, and they both prayed and told me the story of Abraham, who was asked to sacrifice his only son. Like Abraham, I decided to trust and obey God, so I left the kids home in God's care. It was not easy. I cried so much that morning as I was afraid that one of my neighbors would see me leaving without the kids and call child services and I would lose my kids.

When I left that morning to go where God wanted me to be, my children were still in bed, but when I came back home, I ran into their room to make sure that they were okay and to tell them how much I missed them. Of course they thought I was insane! They told me, "Missing is when you are not here. You were just in our room." I then asked them what they ate, and to my astonishment, a few of the things they mentioned I did not have in the pantry and what I had was untouched.

What I learned that day was that God wants a relationship with us based on trust. It is often said, "Let go and let God." This simply means we cannot be in control of our situation if we want God to move in our lives. Any attempt on our part to maintain control is to limit or control God. If we are trying to control God, what do you think he is going to do? Rather than leave the relationship entirely, he may initiate a period of separation or absence so we can learn that we have to surrender or we have to let go of control. He wants us to trust him completely and totally. Remember the Bible warns us in James 1:6–8 that a person who doubts is double minded and unstable in all his ways. But at the same time, God understands our doubt, and the most important thing is that he wants to take it away and increase our faith. Do you remember Thomas in John 20:25–28? Thomas doubted that Christ was indeed risen. He asked for evidence before he could believe. When doubts come, let us not let them take root in our souls. Instead let us turn them over to Christ, and most of all let us saturate our hearts and minds every day with the truths of God's Word, the Bible.

Deal with doubts in faith. We stand on the sure foundation of God's trustworthy Word and his divine Son. Satan will try to turn us away, but in Christ we have this hope as an anchor for the soul firm and secure (Hebrews 6:19). God has given us direction as to how we can determine his voice: the confirmation of his written words. Everything God says will agree with his written Word. Isaiah 8:20 gives us the test to discern error. Any teaching that is not in agreement with God's Word is error and has no light in it.

When doubts arise about your faith, what practical things can you do? Be prepared for your doubts. Doubt is part of Satan's strategy for paralyzing and crippling your faith and preventing your use by God. People often doubt if they are really hearing from God until they learn that God's way is their way. God uses lots of ways to talk to you. Many times God will use other people to talk to you. Don't let doubt litter your mind and ruin your faith.

Be realistic about your doubts. Your doubts and questions about God often come from asking questions whose answers you cannot understand. You want to know more about the nature of God or his eternal plan and why or how this crisis fits into it. But your minds are finite and fallen. You want to know more than you can comprehend. If you can comprehend it, it's not God. Remember, faith is a relationship with God. So be realistic about your doubts. Do you question what you cannot humanly comprehend?

Be honest about your doubts. The only doubt that does permanent damage is the one you won't admit. Isaiah 1:18 in the original Hebrew records God's invitation: "Come, let's argue it out." God knows your questions, your doubts, and your struggles.

Be biblical about your doubts. Judge what you don't know by what you do know. God's Word is true, and Jesus is his Son and your Savior. Find the help of God's Word and his Son for your doubts, your questions, and your problems. Don't let the doubt linger and fester in your mind. Bring it into the light of God's Word. It is easy to have faith when everything makes sense. It is difficult and painful to trust God and live for him when things don't seem to add up. Like Abram was called to go to a new place, God will call you to leave your comfort zone to go to a new duty station. God's will is not an itinerary for the future or a road map for your life. His will is a relationship. His will is stamped all over the Scriptures to transform you into his character (see Matthew 6:33).

Abraham's call was to go to Canaan. What is God's call upon your life? What spiritual journey have you been called to? Being faithful requires that we give up a lot of things. In other words, it requires us to make a sacrifice, and sacrifice develops faith.

CHAPTER 15

An Encounter with the Devil

Be alert and of sober mind. Your enemy the devil prowls around like a roaring lion looking for someone to devour. (1 Peter 5:8 NIV)

It was just an ordinary Sunday, a day my friend and I had chosen to fast and pray. It was not the first time we had done this. She would call me every hour on the hour for us to pray and would break the fast at 4:00 p.m. That day I was not able to get in touch with her. Each time I tried to reach her, my call would go into voice mail, but what I did not know is that my friend was having the same problem. At 4:00 p.m. I tried calling my friend Angela and was relieved when I heard her voice on the other end. She told me that she too had been trying to reach me all day and her calls were going straight into my voice mail.

After talking for a short while, we both realized that the Devil was responsible for our phone problems. You see, dear readers, this was not the first time the Devil had interfered with the phone signals. But we were not prepared for what happened next. He *spoke!* Yes he did. He put my friend's phone on mute and spoke directly to me in her voice. Many hurtful things were said to me, and sad to say I believed it was my dear friend who was being mean. This situation almost brought a rift between us.

My friend Angela was also subjected to the same thing. The Devil put my phone on mute and addressed my friend in my voice. He called her names and cursed her. He revealed to her that he had prepared three men to brutally rape and perform vile acts of violence to her. But my friend knew it was not me, and she began to pray, sing, and read from the Word, rebuking him in the name of Jesus. What he did not tell her was the date that this would take place. But praise God, the all-knowing and powerful God revealed the date to a child. One morning I noticed on my daughter's school calendar that she had circled

November 1 in red and wrote a note. The note said, "Mommy's friend Angela will get into big trouble on this day." I asked her if she wrote the note and what it meant. She told me that three men would "beat Angela up that day."

Once I told my friend the date, she did the only thing that she knew to do: *pray*. She also engaged as many people as she could to join her in prayer, including her parents. John 10:10 tells us that the thief (Devil) came to steal, kill, and destroy. Dear readers, *do not play with the Devil*. If he cannot steal you away from Jesus, he will kill you. If he cannot steal or kill you, he will seek to destroy you. As followers of Jesus in these last days before his second coming, it is imperative to always be alert, for the devil is like a roaring lion seeking whom he may devour. I became very concerned for my friend as November 1 drew near. I am not quite sure how she felt. She never showed fear but continued on in prayer and fasting. She always assured me that she was fine and that her life was in God's hand.

On November 1 God revealed to me that the three men were at the train station my friend got off. When my friend got off from work as she walked the streets, I saw that she was accompanied by an angel. What was more amazing was that her train did not stop at that station where the three men were. That day a victory was gained, and I learned that in the midst of all your trouble, God is right there. He is ready, willing, and more than able to reach out and touch you. The Devil will tell you that God doesn't care, and he won't hear you. He will tell you that you will never be delivered from your present circumstances and you will never receive any peace from the turmoil you are in. These are all lies of the Devil; God is a good God, so don't believe anything to the contrary. If you are sick, God will heal you. If you are having a financial struggle, God will meet that need. No matter the type of satanic attack you are under, God cares and wants to help.

Remember, the Devil is not after your weaknesses, but he is after your strengths. However, he uses your weaknesses to get to your strengths. You must remember that it is a war you are fighting, and Satan, the Enemy, is going to go all out to try to win the battle. Right now he is monitoring your every move to determine how to attack you, to defeat you. He has been studying you ever since you were born, and he knows what you have said, what we have done, and what you do when you think no one is looking. He has assigned his best demons to you, choosing them based on your personal weaknesses and their greatest strengths. First off, the Devil will use your own strengths against you as some of the martial arts do in self-defense.

Pride is the Devil's greatest sin because he thinks he is equal to God, as do a lot of people today. But Satan is only a created creature. So don't fall for his trap; you are a child of God, no matter how much you know or don't know. And remember,

Satan will *always* outwit you with his knowledge because he has a superior intellect, no matter how smart you think you are. *But* since Satan doesn't have a heart and is full of pride, if your thoughts and actions come from a humble heart, you will beat him every time, in Christ Jesus.

Depression is the Devil's compensation for living for him and not for God. He will whisper to you that you are no good, and you might as well end it all now because God will never forgive you since you let him down so much. Of course, before you sin, he will whisper in your ear that you have had a rough life, and you deserve a little pleasure in life. And besides, God will always forgive you. So what's the big deal? So many people fall for this depression trap and commit suicide as a result. *Don't be fooled.* God will *always* forgive you if you repent. And always remember that Satan can show people a great physical time, for a while. He will give people money, sex, power, or whatever to convince them that they have the secret of life. But he will *always* pop your balloon after he has blown it up and puffed you up with pride. The Bible says, "It is impossible to please God if you live in the flesh" (Romans 8:8).

Another strategy of his is to always upset you so that you will start to question why God allows these bad things to happen to you. *After all*, you will start to think, *I am a good person, and if God loved me, then he wouldn't let these things happen to me.* Well, guess what? None of the saints ever lived perfect.

Read Job 38 if you want the answer to this question! This is why we must always be alert because we have an adversary in the Devil, and we are engaged in spiritual combat. With any war there are casualties. God may not always deliver you from the fiery furnace, but he will deliver you from the hand of the enemy.

Remember, the more you commit yourself to Christ, the more demons Satan will assign to you to trip you up. But they have no power over you *unless* you give in to their temptations. So always remember that you have two choices in life: either your body can drag your soul to hell *or* your soul can lift your body to heaven. *Choose wisely!* The psalmist wrote, "It is good to be near God" (Psalm 73:28 NIV). Jesus said, "No one can come to me unless the Father who sent me draws them; and I will raise them up at the last day" (John 6:44 NIV). God says, "After I called you, I expect you from then on to exercise initiative in seeking to draw near to me." If you do, you have this very encouraging promise: "Come near to God and He will come near to you" (James 4:8 NIV).

Angela and I know that we can never turn back. As of the writing of this book, my friend Angela is preparing to go into the seminary. As for me, God is my shield and my fortress, and he will not let my enemies triumph over me (Psalm 25:2).

CHAPTER 16

My Bed of Affliction

I will be glad and rejoice in your love for you
saw my affliction and knew the anguish of my
soul. (Psalm 31:7 NIV)

I am in love with God because he is friendly, humble, loving,
merciful, just, smart, and compassionate; I can go on and on,
but there will not be enough paper and ink to pen who God
is. God is like a giant onion, and each layer represents one
trait in his character. You have to experience him to know
him. One thing that I discover about pain and suffering is
that sometimes God allows it not because you deserve it or

because of your sins but because the Devil challenged him for your love and loyalty. God allows it because he is sure of his relationship with you.

One Friday night I was on the phone with my friend Angela, and I began to feel ill. I told her that I did not feel good and that I could not describe it. I just knew that something was wrong. Immediately I started to cough, which I did for about twenty minutes nonstop. Next I felt like I was on fire, and my body started to ache. Angela prayed with me and insisted that this was from the Devil himself. She stayed on the phone with me until 11:00 p.m. All this started around 9:00 p.m. on that Friday night. After I got off the phone with my friend, things got really bad, and I did not sleep that night. By Saturday morning I was paralyzed. I could not feel my legs, and I could not turn or move. My head felt like a cement truck ran over it. I was on my back in a literal bed of affliction. I cried out to God to come and deliver me, but he did not come.

The following morning around 6:00 a.m., Angela called me to see how I was doing. I told her there was no change and I was unable to sleep during the night. She again insisted this was from the Devil and that she was coming over to pray and anoint me. On her way to the bus stop, my friend received a text instructing her not to come over and not to worry. The text further said that I was suffering because of my faith because the Devil rejected God's view of my character. My friend tried to tell me the message in the text, but the only part I could hear was, "God told me not to come and not to worry." Angela and another friend tried to stay connected via telephone, encouraging me through out that day. I was in so much pain that I cried for hours, and my two friends cried also as they prayed with me.

I got frantic when my daughter told me that my son's blood sugar was 50. I had my daughter bring me a bottle of juice to give to my son, but I could not open it, and neither could she. My heart was truly broken that day because I could not care for my children. That's when the Devil began to taunt me. He told me that I was going to jail because my children were dead in the other room. Meanwhile, I called for my children, but they did not come. I did not hear or see them all day. The Devil began to tell me that they were dead and I was going to jail. I began to believe they were dead. I told Angela that the kids were dead, but she assured me that was not the case, and even if it that was the case, I must believe that God was able to raise them up again.

The Devil has a filthy mouth that only speaks profanity. When my two friends got on the phone, he taunted them too. He told Angela she was going to jail because the children were in the next room dying and she would not even come over to help. They began to pray. At that time God sent one of my two friends a text that simply said, "Remember the story of Job."

This situation went on all day Saturday. I was not able to get up to eat, drink, take a shower, or even use the bathroom. I urinated in the bed, so now I was in pain, paralyzed, and lying in a bed of urine and believing that my two kids were dead. I cried and cried until my eyes were swollen.

Then around 10:00 p.m. that Saturday night I said, "Enough is enough." With all the strength I could muster, I began to rebuke that Devil, and then I declared my undying love to God. I began to sing praises to God like there was no tomorrow. I told the Devil that I did not care if I lived or died, but I would never serve him; and even if the kids were dead and he took my life, I would be in heaven when Jesus came so he could go to hell where he belonged and burn forever. I rebuked him in the name of Jesus, my Savior. What I did not know was that God had dialed Angela's phone, and she and my other friend, Joanne, heard everything. Yes he did because I did not call her and I was not on the phone. She said her phone rang at around 10:00 p.m., and she thought it was me but they realized I was not on the phone. She also received a text at 12:58 a.m. that said, "Do you see what I mean? She is so faithful. Call her. It is over."

At midnight God came into my room and said, "My child, it is over," and I was immediately fully restored, after twenty-seven hours of excruciating pain. I arose from that bed, went to my children's room, and saw that they were alive and well and sleeping peacefully. I then proceeded to change the wet linen from my bed and do the laundry. I was up until three o'clock Sunday morning doing the laundry. But I was glad to be alive, and like the Psalmist said, I rejoiced in God's love for he saw my affliction and he knew the anguish of my soul, but he did not forsake me.

Yes God's ways are not always easy to understand. Sometimes we never do, and that is why I trust God with everything I have. I trust him with my children, my health, my money, and my life. Friends, it is not an easy road, but you can walk that road by faith. Do not choose comfort over God. God wants to talk to you. He wants to laugh and cry with you simply because he loves you. Why don't you give him a try? Allow him to rekindle your love for him again, and if you are like me and never knew him, give him a try today. He makes the difference. In fact, God is the difference between life and death.

CHAPTER 17

God's Steadfast Promises

The Bible is filled with promises God made to us. These promises are as sure as the one who made them, and God wants us to claim his promises. These words have brought comfort to many throughout the ages, and I hope these promises will give you comfort and peace as you await God's deliverance.

In Jeremiah 29:11 God promised us that he has plans for each of us: "'For I know the plans I have for you,' declares the Lord. 'Plans to prosper you and not to harm you, plans to give you hope and a future'" (NIV). Friends, never give up, God will see you through. If you are in need, God has promised to take care of your needs in Philippians 4:19: "And my God will meet all your needs according to the riches of his glory in Christ Jesus" (NIV).

If you are tired and struggling because you have too much to deal with, God can give you rest, and he has promised to do this if you allow him. God extends a warm and cordial invitation to each of you: "Come to me, all you who are weary and burdened, and I will give you rest. Take my yoke upon you and learn from me, for I am gentle and humble in heart, and you will find rest for your souls" (Matthew 11:28–29 NIV). God loves his people, and this is the major reason why he freed the Israelites from that terrible yoke in Egypt. Today as well, he loves you and wants to free you from any bondages in your life. All you need to do is agree to enter into a relationship with your heavenly Father. God is faithful!

Zephaniah 3:17 tells us, "The Lord your God is with you, the Mighty Warrior who saves. He will take great delight in you; in his love he will no longer rebuke you, but will rejoice over you with singing" (NIV). What a powerful promise from a God who wants to have a relationship with you. You are never alone!

John 15:13–17 says:

> Greater love has no one than this: to lay down one's life for one's friends. You are my friends if you do what I command. I no longer call

you servants, because a servant does not know his master's business. Instead, I have called you friends, for everything that I learned from my Father I have made known to you. (NIV)

The greatest proof that God wants to have intimacy with you is found in these texts! God came down from heaven to reestablish that relationship with you and me. Sin had brought separation between God and his children, but Jesus reestablished that connection. Isaiah 59:2 tells us that our sins have separated us from God, so that he will not hear. We chose a path of self-destruction, but God cared so much for us he made it possible for us to get to know him again as our Father and Redeemer.

Hebrews 13:8 says, "Jesus Christ is the same yesterday and today and forever" (NIV). He will never change! God is saying to us, "I loved you yesterday! I love you today, and I will still love you tomorrow!" Those who cannot appreciate relationships do not know God, for he is a God of relationships! We are not the ones who first loved God, but it is clearly God who first loved us and pursues intimacy with us. Knowing this, how can you do anything but "love one another" as Jesus commanded us?

You may be a victim of domestic abuse and feel like there is no way out of your situation. Maybe your situation is so desperate that it makes you feel helpless and powerless. If so, claim the promise God made to you in Isaiah 40:29–31:

> He gives strength to the weary and increases the power of the weak. Even youths grow tired and weary, and young men stumble and fall; but those who hope in the Lord will renew their strength. They will soar on wings like eagles; they will run and not grow weary, they will walk and not be faint. (NIV)

Domestic violence is a serious issue that affects mostly women and children. Don't let despair keep you down; you were made to soar like eagles. Allow God to renew your strength so you can take flight like an eagle.

God has promised in Proverbs 1:33 that all who listen to me will live in peace, untroubled by fear of harm. And finally he has promised us a gift: "I am leaving you with a gift—peace of mind and heart. And the peace I give is a gift the world cannot give. So don't be troubled or afraid" (John 14:27).

These promises of God are powerful, and I hope they will be helpful to you no matter what your situation may be. Be strong; God is only a prayer away, and God certainly does deliver.